CADUCEUS

Gabriel Griffin

First published 2023 by The Hedgehog Poetry Press

Published in the UK by
The Hedgehog Poetry Press
Coppack House, 5
Churchill Avenue
Clevedon
BS21 6QW

www.hedgehogpress.co.uk

ISBN: 978-1-916830-06-6

9 8 7 6 5 4 3 2 1

A CIP Catalogue record for this book is available from the British Library.

Photo of Gabriel Griffin by Alessio Zanelli

Introduction

If a poetic Fairy Godmother offered you three wishes, what would you ask for? To find a publisher who would catapult you to fame? To write like (fill in the name)? To produce a few outstanding poems – or even just one? Or to ...? Where does one start? Rather than struggling to choose between specifics, I might opt for more general priorities: to get better at seeing, saying and shaping.

By 'seeing' I mean really perceiving, through my own eyes, what it is that I am looking at; at seeing similarities and differences, connections and implications. Looking, in one sense or another, is crucial, but just looking is not enough. I love looking at mountains, but that alone doesn't get me very far towards a poem.

'Saying' means not just saying what I perceive, but having a reason: who do I want to tell, and why, and what might this bring to them? Things must be worth sharing. Telling you simply that my lover is like a delicate flower may not add much to your personal development.

Most of all I would want to be better at 'shaping' – at finding the words, and arrangements of words, that might turn what I have to say into poetry. The nature of such words and arrangements is impossible to define, but we know it when we find it. It is what can sometimes make a line of a poem mysteriously raise the hairs on the back of your neck.

In the absence of a Fairy Godmother, one can learn a good deal about such things from other poets. Fortunately, if I am looking for guidance, I don't need to go far: Gabriel Griffin's collection offers lessons in excellence in all three areas. What she sees is always perceived in the light of her individual experience and beliefs; what she says invariably brings us something valuable; every communication is skilfully shaped. Perhaps one test of a good poem is: could anyone else have seen and said things in this way? Never in Griffin's case.

The children playing in the lava fields of a partly active volcano (*The children of Stromboli*) are strikingly observed and described; but at the same time we are shown that their carefree games bring them "close to the ticking, the tolling heartbeat of the earth", the massive destructive force of the "living Cyclops underground". The observation and the reflection run parallel; neither is a platform for the other.

In *Nicotiana*, a visually compelling portrayal of tobacco harvesters leads into, but is not replaced by, a disturbing comparison of shrivelling tobacco leaves with shrivelling hands. And this turns to a more terrifying thought about how a young smoker's lungs might flake and deteriorate, as the 'cow-lung pink' tobacco flowers will.

At the other end of the emotional spectrum, two charming poems celebrate a refusal to see things the way one is supposed to. In *Heedless* Griffin ignores someone's decree that she should pray respectfully to the water as if it were a temple. "I forget! Here I am, / feet first in the spray, / soaking wet, tossing / water, hugged / by invisible gods, playing / a game even older / than they." In *The Nuns' Araucaria* a monkey-puzzle tree remains anarchically out of place in an obsessively tidied-up convent garden, its giant fingers "effing up at the skies". And perhaps (Griffin speculates) the nuns sneak naughtily out at night, strip out of their cumbersome habits and climb up naked towards "the winking stars".

Water shows up frequently. While this is not surprising – Griffin has spent much of her life on an island in a lake – there is nothing at all predictable about water's presence in her poetry. In *Well* it is dark and silent: "Reflected in the dark / – or lying far below – was / nobody I seem to know." The underground water in *Cistern* is a frightening element which stands in contrast with the town's fresh-flowing fountains, but it is equally a refuge from the blood that flows from the appalling ritual animal slaughter going on above. *Learning to read the lake*, one of Griffin's finest poems, begins with a beautifully expressed account of how she was taught to interpret and respond to the messages written by the different winds on the "open pages of the lake". Then the same extended metaphor returns at a second level, as she reveals what is now happening to her teacher, on whose face worries, hidden thoughts and fears write similar messages. "On your parchment face / is written love in cursive, loss / in strokes ..." In another poem, the sad and deeply moving *Lament for an illegal immigrant*, water is fully personified, as a participant which joins in nature's song of rage and grief.

Dryness is naturally a concern. The fire that lurks underground in *The children of Stromboli* comes to the surface in *The oleander once a garden*.

Et in Arcadia ego shows the aftermath of the devastating fires of 2007 that destroyed a beloved landscape. Dryness becomes a heartbreaking personal image in *Golem*, where a sufferer from dementia has become a parched and lost person. "I wish you rain / to quench your thirst and stars / to guide you back again. Because / what you've left here is just / a husk you once quickened / with your name."

Gods, mythical figures and legends have a place in Griffin's world: there are incidental references to Hermes, the Cyclops, a reflected Medusa, a Hindu temple, belief in werewolves, and more. Pan is an important figure in *Et in Arcadia ego*. This complex and intriguing poem expresses much of Griffin's perception of life and nature as double-sided and ambiguous, of a world where things are both where they belong and not where they belong, both what they seem and not what they seem, both what they have been and not what they have been. "Past and future shimmered / through a mask of shifting water; myth, art, life, love – / at times some glimmer will survive." Another mythical figure provides the symbol on which the title poem *Caduceus* builds, as she addresses once again, from a new angle, the impossibility of seeing nature and relationships in simple terms.

Although the transience and uncertainty of relationships is a recurrent topic, Griffin is not at all a confessional poet. Her poems tell us what she wants to tell us, no less and no more. Any back story, though hinted at, is not generally our business. One engaging poem, *Sleeping not weeping*, touches, only half-humorously, on a relationship which didn't develop. "Your death-day went unmarked by me ... Silent, you left me / bereft of memories, of all the years / we never had ... And I ... never felt a thing."

Outsiders looks at the kind of boulders that turn up far from their natural geological setting, brought down from the mountains by glacier movement or erosion. Though out of place, they are more or less settled in their new homes despite their "alien forms". But they too hint at their back stories: "still each molecule bears a memory / of feldspar, mica, quartz, / and glitters in a rare sun." The poem itself is an apparent outsider, standing apart from the general run of the collection. But is it really an outsider, or is its author saying something important about herself and and all of us? Well, the poem tells us what it wants to tell us.

Griffin uses a fair amount of internal rhyme and assonance: not enough to obtrude, but enough to support her expertise in choosing and sequencing words. "Heat / shimmers the scene unreal; a card discarded from / a faded pack, its colours smudged and blurring". At the structural level, she is adept at balancing and contrasting the literal and the metaphorical; and where technical skill supports deep emotional commitment, as in the extended metaphors of *Learning to read the lake* or *Lament for an illegal immigrant*, the result is poetry of great power.

This is a very fine small collection by a poet who deserves to be much better known. Perhaps she wonders, as many of us do, "What is my work really worth in the overall scheme of things? Would contemporary literature be any the poorer without my poems?" I believe it certainly would. If this sounds extravagant, go and read *Lament for an illegal immigrant.*

Michael Swan

Contents

Nicotiana tabacum.L

". . . a viscid annual or short-lived perennial"

In Umbrian fields, stooping, tanned, straw
hats over cotton fazzoletti, they slowly pan
down lines of green, the flowers cow-lung
pink clustered in a brazen showing. Heat
shimmers the scene unreal, a card discarded from
a faded pack, its colours smudged and blurring.
On a shaded terrace we pour cool wine, gaze
while they heap the baskets, carts, and straighten
sighing, take the loads in lines to sheds,
seeds of sweat and tiredness shining.

*

No, thanks, I don't! Leaves shrivel, twist,
contract like hands whose fingers yellowing
lose lymph, as they their cool ellipses.
Heat swirls the smoke haze of the shed,
in the darkening day, a choking, bitter scent.

*

You cultivate flowers of your own, their petals
soft as ash, flyaway as clocks of dandelions.
Cut it out! Or down, at least. You're young . . .
You laugh, inhale, breathe blossoms newly blown
whorled, impalpable, feathery as down.
I close my eyes, see petals flake, fall, form
loam where spores seed, mycelia creep
and black fungi slowly grow.

Outsiders

You don't always notice them. The thorn
and tangle of years has smudged
their alien forms, but there –

under the berries and briar, the lizards'
flickering, a slow-worm curled easily
in their bulks' dark hollow – they urge

their granite stolidity, their right
to stay where they rest. No return now
to the arid slopes, the mountain's

sterility, the wind's hard blowing. Too
ponderous to go further, the force
that had driven them spent, deposited

in an alien land, dull in leaves' shadow,
still each molecule bears a memory
of feldspar, mica, quartz,

and glitters in a rare sun.

Lament for an illegal immigrant

No moon, but fishermen
are used to that and the sea's chanting,
the descant of the nets. The decks
silvered with sea verses,
the minims and trebles of fish
hushed into songbooks of ice.

Something didn't sing, humped
in the net, thudding onto the deck.
Its ears heard no notes, its eyes blind
to the men standing by, its throat
choked with words
that no one would hear.

They let the sly octopus
sidle to the ship's side, forgot to stop
the arch and leap of bream.
The sea moaned, the fish
slipped out of tune, the kittiwakes
hurled screeches like broken strings.

The men unfroze, thumped
what didn't sing, what was lost for words,
over the hissing deck. Tipped that which
had no hope, had never had a hope,
back to the sea. No
word, no hymn, no prayer.

But the wrack in the nets wept. The sea
beat its fists on the boat. And the wind got up
and howled till dawn.

Panic

Before I came
you thought to close
the shutters against the spying
night and if
the wind rose.

Before I came
you went outside, around
the house alone, shutting out
the surf sigh on the rocks, the scent
of smoke from over – where? –
the caper petals staining pink,
the goat.

You shut, shut, shut, locked in
the light, the joss-sticks' glow, the sequinned
wine, a still, bright
gecko on the wall, the silky shine
of cushions waiting soft, the candles
flamed, the sitar on the CD low.

Before I came
you'd lost yourself outside, caught
in an antique dark, a starless
maze, a pagan
game, a Mediterranean
night.

Before I came
you'd gone

Ropes

She went down to the harbour most days,
checked on the boat from the quay,
controlled the ropes coiled in their careful loops
tight with a winter's salt, noted the paint
flaking like whispered words and how
the mast seemed a lone thing,
a long-boned beast, a jumper

tied by one leg, and only its dreams flaring,
sparking light over the storytelling sea.
Gulls screamed down the weather, tea-light
swilled on the flags. She smiled the door shut,
cast off sour wool, tried to sleek
the restless goading of brine.

Staring at the window, his eyes were
winter water, his skin anything bleached
too high for the tide. Her name in his mouth
was a knot, pulling cords fretted with habit.
At night they were algae, shape-shifting
in black waters, slipping out of embraces.

She goes down to the harbour most days, looks
from the empty mooring, sees in her mind the ketch
leaping free over the sea, hears words
painted bright over blanched thought, and knows
his eyes have soaked up sea colours, his voice
rides hard on the wind, and he's untied
her name.

Heedless

Something I'd
never thought about, had always
rushed in, careful only
of rocks and weeds and
things that nipped or bit or
caught at my toes or
slipped round in a slimy
way. You said
to pray –

pray? Pray. Show
respect. Let
your hands not your feet
greet the waves, give
thanks; enter the tide
like a temple. Hindu.

I always mean
to remember, to do
as you say, to pray –

I forget! Here I am
feet first in the spray,
soaking wet, tossing
water, hugged
by invisible gods, playing
a game even older
than they.

River flowering

in memoriam Y. C.

If you'd been here, would things
have changed? The winter river
spilling out to sea, the swell
on the point of freeze, the salt air
licking tears? You'd have heard
the drawn-out groans of phantom boats,
a chill moan from a sax – it goes,

fog choked. Would you have seen
there on the jetty wall, blurred colours
fading in the mist, her skirt a swirl
of dying blooms around thin legs?
The watchman shivering in his coat, pointed
here – *no, there!* – a wavering beam of light.
She's gone – could *you*
have stopped her?

The watchman said in court he'd never
guessed, he'd no idea she'd be
doing what she did. Had *you?*
He hadn't seen the rest (you
didn't know), the squalid room, that old
fat lecher in her bed, the bloated belly
blubber on her drawn skin, her eager mind
pricked beyond her finest reasoning.
Her eyes could see only what he played,
the acid trumps, the jumbled hands
of his infernal game.

It must have been like this: he turned
and slept, she rose. To halt
the frenetic shuffling in her mind, to stifle
howling orange and shrieking red, dilute
acid violet and sour mauve, she
could only think
to sluice the cold grey river
right through her petalled head.

Don't blame yourself. Like
the watchman, you couldn't know
or stop her. Just look, one last time, over there,
see through the mist flowers
fade on an ebbing tide, and she become
a cuttlebone, a pale thin fish, then
seabird, white-winged, wind-spinning,
crying out to sea – do you hear? –
Begin again, begin again!

The Children of Stromboli

are quick as hares in cane-beds, their bare feet
winged by Hermes, sure they can outrace

sluggish streams of lava, streak over red-hot coals.
Hounding the chypre and almond scent of fig trees

they split thieved fruits with dirty nails and, sticky still
with sweetness, scratch out mushrooms in the loam.

Abandoning the swishing bamboo
to the sighing sounds of sea-wind, they

race down sullen slopes to black beaches
shouting, scuffling over ashen sands to build

not castles, but volcanoes. Moulding cones
with small and smutty fingers, they stuff

craters with dry grasses, then, breath caught,
apply (forbidden) lighters, blow, bet cents

on which will burn the longest, whose
volcano flames the most.

The children of Stromboli play hide 'n seek
in sulphurous caverns, theirs lairs wombs of darkness

close to the ticking, the tolling, the heartbeat
of the earth. They are aware but unbothered

by the livid Cyclops underground, half-asleep
in molten lava – half-sleeping, half-awake.

Golem

Sometimes you lose
your name. I call

but you've gone. All you've left
are muscles, skin, a golem

fully working but – not you.
You've flown, you've gone

hunting flying thoughts,
your slanting swift's wings eyes

spy hidden lands, you're searching hard
for nests long tumbled into dust,

questing through thick clouds
of memories you never had,

blown by winds of words
you can no longer understand.

I wish you rain
to quench your thirst and stars

to guide you back again. Because
what you've left here is just a husk

you once quickened with your name.
I call and call . . .

Sleeping, not weeping

Your death-day went unmarked by me.
I lit no candle, shed no tear, no
fear had chilled me, no plucking from afar

of common chords, no web of threads
shook, shivered, tore. You sent
no messenger, cast no shade before

sighed no scented breath across
my tangled hair. Silent, you left me
bereft of memories, of all the years

we never had, of laughing lies, of truthful
tears, your hand withdrawn, unfelt,
from mine. And I – despite my cards, my

crystal ball, my ESP, my pendulum
(that ring you gave me years ago)
never felt a thing.

Web-weaver

She'd always lied. Her perfidy
shone sugar-coated, sticky threads
of sweet-tongued fabrication
hardening to steel. She span a web
of falsehood, on which words stuck and swung
while, mesmerized, we watched her
dance down the trembling lines
– and pounce.

We vowed revenge, we'd
"get 'er!" But, as from a craftwork
lampshade – string, glue, balloon – light
escapes through windows in the net, she slipped
out of the tangled web she'd spun. She left
only the outline of the self we thought
we'd known. We searched, but when the sun
slashed through the frame of lies, we found
just random lines upon the ground
scattered runes that none of us can understand.

Learning to read the lake

You taught me the language of the lake. To know
from the fender's thud against the boat, the frizzle
spiralling down the birch, the thrumming

of the palm, which wind will soon
scribble its name across
the open pages of the lake, if we

should fasten the moorings and lock
the shutters close –
or hoist sail and razor through

the colours of the sky. And hear
the bow whine drawn across a saw
of swan wings, with their background beat.

To read, as well, its changing lines.
The precise calligraphy of the south wind
marking short, tight strokes, the bold

slashes of tramontana, the curling loops
a rare west wind scrawls across the lake
the wayward doodles of the crazy Cus.

And its notes: the eye ripples of the plunging grebe,
the deltas drawn by moorhens, the points of light
stippled by oars at dusk.

*

Now I am learning your language, too.
The quick shirring worry pulls
beneath the clear surface of your skin,

the curling scribbling
of untranslated thought, the sudden
thrum of your fears. On your parchment face

is written love in cursive, loss
in strokes. I will not read the gothic hand,
I fear it is prophecy.

Your thoughts plunge beneath
the chill surface of your skin. I wait, praying
for ripples of light in the dusk.

Et in Arcadia Ego

'Here werewolves fed on human flesh'. We shivered, it was
dusk and none unwise enough to creep about these
antique tombs except the rats and us. Summer tourists
had flown home months back, we'd thought to find
Arcadia's pleasant fields, its groves, its lines of verse,

shepherds with their pipes, a nymph, perhaps – not this,
the blackened bones of trees, ash altars, crackling scrub.
It seemed that nothing lived, a hoary veil had dropped shrouding
land and art and myth. *Et in Arcadia ego* – did it mean
in death? Like Pan, the great god Pan, who once ran

free and wild in just these groves, drunk on wine
from the same twisted vines whose lymph has now been dried
by devastating fires. Pan dead – and all Arcadia
died, the shadows crept like werewolves close. 'Let's
go,' I said, and, turning, dropped the guide. I stooped

to fish it from the ash, and spotted close beside
a minute plant with green leaves and what seemed
swollen buds. So something was alive
in all this wasteland! I had no idea what plant it was
but no harm surely to take one sprig, a good luck sign

to ward off marble death. I broke off
a stem – and fell back in surprise, my face was
dripping wet, a liquid jet had been directed to my eyes
by that small offended plant. Past and future shimmered
through a mask of shifting water: myth, art, life, love –
at times some glimmer may survive.

Cistern

Turks don't like
still water. In time they forgot
it was there, heavy, silent, pressing
under the quick streets, the fretted palace,
the sky-painted mosques; the fountains
threading silver sounds through the sun,
light voices running in the shade.

The cooks were mute, slipping onto painted plates
blind white carp bought from one who knew
his way in the watery dark, dared to row
through the clammy maze of columns
dodging the Medusa's stare, looped
in the chill vapours of the sunless damp.

*

When the slaughter began, I ran
through the shouting crowds, past carts
of green cucumbers, spiced cakes, popcorn, baked
potatoes, choking smoke from black grills
toasting sausages, kebabs, pink
floppy flesh, plunged

down the steps, slipping on green slime
of vaults fifteen hundred years dark
into an antique silence away
from the screams of the dying, the butchers'
laughter, the crimson trickle in the gutter.

Pale fish slid under my feet, weaving a net
amber and black. I stepped over the water
hunting the Medusa, found her reversed, her eyes
reflecting Time's waste. Should I stay, my life
turning to stone in an underground world?
Or return, to the run and flow of blood
in the festive streets?

The oleander once a garden

Where oleanders scrawled over the hill falling
from the ruined wasn't a castle but could've been in spite
of idiot pictures splattered over the upstairs no-stairs walls
and the boys didn't do them – they swore.

Where they went from their first motorbikes in
ecstasy and summer and the roar was the giant
droning of bees in the burred heat and their girls
laughed through hairwebs woven of wind and fright.

Where they scattered books over the grass printing
spiders inky and leggy between the unturned unread
pages and the heat slipped under the net of stalks
pricking uncounted the numbered days.

Where they thought it was forever in the never
never was a garden and each kiss was a petal fallen
from a soft-footed thief of a summer running off
with colours stolen from their dreams.

Where they were unaware of the oleanders burning
brown around the edges, the empty windows, broken
stairs, obscene scenes, and turned too late to see
hills flare, the cobalt dome tilt, tip, spin into a wheel of fire.

Where the summer smashed into a kaleidoscope
of broken metal banging against their futures, shattering
the rosy petals, the fine entanglements of stalk and web,
crushing the careful calligraphy into clay.

Where in the glimmering air the garden which never was
rose with the could've been castle like a kite slipped forever
from their grasp to wander in the empty vaults of their futures,
trailing petals and scents down the years

where they aren't any more. There.

Well

An iron moon. The rust
had nibbled at the lock years past,
my hands were drawn in ruddy lines

of hearts and heads and smeary mounds
of rubbled destinies – *not mine*. I shoved
the lot aside. Some other time . . .

Below, a watchful dark. Thin threads
of slime coiled round the stone, a sigh –
or was it mine? – exhaled

and quivered, though the black
remained quite still. So what
for daytime stars? The Pleiades,

Orion – just tales, I bet, folklore
at best. These waters
swallow light. A shiver

(damp, of course!) ran up
the well. I leaned across the sill
a last time, to be sure . . .

reflected in the dark
– or lying far below – was
nobody I seemed to know.

Embryo angel

Something about that seagull didn't click. The others
scrambled, screamed, caught biscuits in their beaks, squabbled
over broken bits, settled on the cold skin of the lake, replete.

This bobbed like all the rest, but though I got the boat out,
didn't rise in blinding flight, a white tornado hurling cries,
wings slashing, slicing light, scattering

shadow blades elusive over freezing waves.
Instead, it swayed – gull ghost, embryo angel, blind
poem, empty prayer – into my naked hands, its eyes ice.

Perfect, it was, the feathers traced like snowflakes seen
in microscopes, the white immaculate, no wound,
no weight. It stayed light on my hand as though

nothing was inside, no tendons, blood or fat,
hollow as that children's toy for floating in the bath,
or the duck nailed – joking figurehead – to Don Giacomo's boat,

a fairground target shot at for a worthless prize, a decoy.
Couldn't have eaten for days, not like the rest who fly
in noisy wheels up past my window, catch crumbs

in mid-air flight, trace spirals and loops against the fading sky
crying – hypocrites! – for far-off cliffs, wind-socked wings,
salt-biting spray.

And it was as though something had flown
out of a buried past, hair feather soft, a look forgotten
years before, a young hand in mine. A memory

light as that gull, empty of what was, hollow inside, all
warmth gone, dried like vapoured ice, pale spider's husk,
a feathered shell, wings folded frozen to its side.

Last light. The lake shines silver, ice-black sky. The flocks
have swooped behind the hills. No bird, no dog howls
at intruding shades, no bell rings the stillness, there's no

boat's ripple, stir. The gull flames through the dusk
to northern gods, a Viking fate. Against night's
tramontana waves, I winch the boat up high.

Kampango and the mouth-brooders

An average of minus five, day after day after day. And only sun
flooding the frosted bridge, washing us in its winter warmth.
We slow, lean on the rail, look down through the waters' gold

while I hold her mittened hand tight. *There!* I say, *See them?*
By the shutters that board up the lake two great fish, fin to fin, sway,
not swimming. *Days, they've been there!* says a local, and points

to the far side of the lake where a vast shoal of young fish
darkens the waters like weeds. *Chub! Just put in. See
them two trout? Keeping watch over their eggs, won't let*

those young 'uns go near 'em! Now we are a shoal
of bystanders and our eyes slipping over the trout
are quick and dark as the chub in their eager hunger. Like

Lake Malawi with its giant catfish, the parents, each a metre long,
guard the eggs in their rock nest under the waters, taking turns
to flip off cichlids anxious to make a meal of the eggs –

and later the minute writhing babes – while women wash
kids and coloured clothes on the banks
and black and white-striped kingfishers dart in the sun.

All day the Kampango, scallop-finned, whiskered like cats,
swish sleepily at the nipping cichlids. Till night throws
its dark net over the waters, catching the cichlids

in a close mesh of sleep. Then Kampango are alert to the hunt
and take turns to slope off for fry, their long white barbels
sensing out the prey. Which often is cichlids, those little, bothering

nuisances of cichlids, who nurse their own babes in their mouths
till they are ready to be spat out
into the devouring mouth of the world.

The Nuns' Araucaria

Not at all the kind of tree you'd expect to find
In a monastery garden. It squears above the wall
Its giant fingers horning the heavens, effing
Up at the skies. And the nuns who moved in have
Left it there, yet chopped down the stammering mimosa,
The cherry whose blossom danced a swan lake
Over the boughs, the sacred yew by the gate with its
Scarlet berries we plucked and sucked and spat at
The monastery well. But a *monkey puzzle?*

Was it an abbot who had planted it, a symbol
Of life's labyrinth or of evil's intricacies? Did he intend it
To stand as a speechless sermon long after he'd died?
Is it a warning of purgatory's trials or a statement
Of the life we are confusedly living, snared, squittering
In Fate's mesh, while the Dark Hunter, unmoved,
Looks on? Or does it symbolize nothing
At all, have no significance, is just a prelate's whim,
A caprice to slip between the lines of the Rule?

From my window at night that tree cavorts
With the stars, tracing the Game of the Goose
Over the mooning sky. Soundless as shadows nuns
Slide under its boughs – who's to tell if it grabs at their veils
Or pricks them on their silent way? Or do they –
For some penance or for a sly joy – clamber
Into its bristly branches, struggle out of their
Caught and cumbersome habits, and wriggle,
Naked and lithe as monkeys, up to the winking stars?

Caduceus

After. Raking through
what you'd said. Banal, and yet –
some phrase not clear, a word
ill-used, a meaning
still obscure –

of course, for sure! It wasn't
one but two – meanings, I mean – a twin
string of words like pearls, like
DNA, a double helix looping
through my brain, two
serpents twining around
my spine, a caduceus
of mixed intent, a promise
to be picked up if . . .

you went. I'm left
trying to recall – how
did that riddle go? – which
of two to ask the way if one
tells the truth, the other lies
and you haven't a clue
who's who?

Acknowledgements

Some of these poems have been published previously by:
Aesthetica, Chalk Face Muse, White Adder; Blinking Eye; Private Photo Review; Ripley; Peterloo; Barnet Borough Arts; Writers' Forum; Norwich Writers; Ceth Uclan; Lit (Romania).

Photo of Gabriel Griffin by Alessio Zanelli

Milton Keynes UK
Ingram Content Group UK Ltd.
UKHW010706220923
429186UK00004B/284

9 781916 830066